The Shark Book

Pamela Chanko

Brought to you by the editors of

My Weekly Reader

Children's Press®
An imprint of Scholastic Inc.

How to Read This Book

This book is for kids and grown-ups to read together—side by side!

A 🙂 means it is the kid's turn to read.

A grown-up can read the rest.

Simple text for kids who are learning to read

Harder text—which builds knowledge and vocabulary— for grown-ups to read aloud

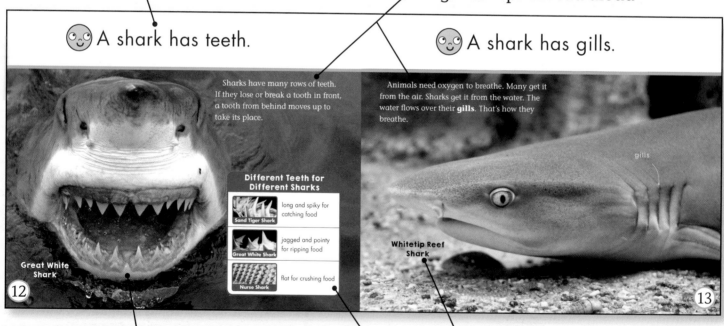

🙂 A shark has teeth.

Sharks have many rows of teeth. If they lose or break a tooth in front, a tooth from behind moves up to take its place.

🙂 A shark has gills.

Animals need oxygen to breathe. Many get it from the air. Sharks get it from the water. The water flows over their **gills**. That's how they breathe.

gills

Different Teeth for Different Sharks

Sand Tiger Shark — long and spiky for catching food

Great White Shark — jagged and pointy for ripping food

Nurse Shark — flat for crushing food

Great White Shark

Whitetip Reef Shark

12

13

Bright photos to talk about

Nonfiction text features like charts and captions

2

Table of Contents

Whale Shark

Mako Shark

Bullhead Shark

Blacktip Reef Shark

Hammerhead Shark

Cookiecutter Shark

Tiger Shark

Chapter 1

All Kinds of Sharks

There are many kinds of sharks. Let's see some up close!

Dogfish Shark

Great White Shark

Angelshark

Catshark

Sharks can be big.

The whale shark is the biggest shark in the world. But it's not dangerous. Its teeth are so tiny you can barely see them! Whale sharks eat **plankton** and very small fish.

Whale Shark

Whale sharks can be 40 feet long or more. That's about as long as a school bus!

Sharks can be small.

The dwarf lanternshark is tiny. It sparkles and glows in the darkness of the deep sea. Twinkle, twinkle, little shark!

Dwarf Lanternshark

The dwarf lanternshark can fit in a person's hand!

Sharks can be wide.

The hammerhead shark has one eye and one **nostril** on each side of its wide head. It swings its head from side to side so it can see and smell in both directions!

nostril

eye

Hammerhead
Shark

Sharks can be long.

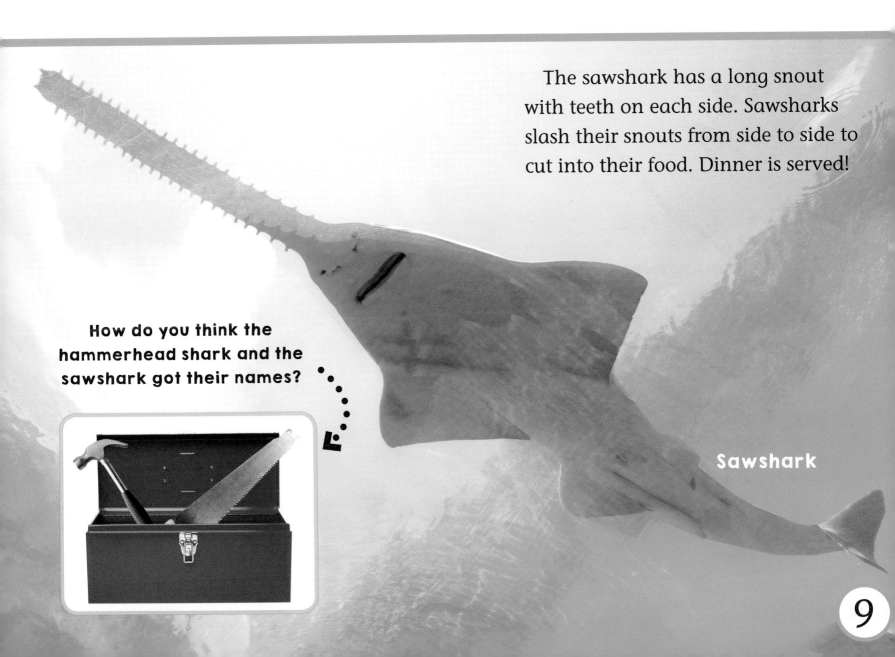

The sawshark has a long snout with teeth on each side. Sawsharks slash their snouts from side to side to cut into their food. Dinner is served!

How do you think the hammerhead shark and the sawshark got their names?

Sawshark

Sharks can be fast!

The great white shark is a fast and fierce hunter. When it spots a meal from below, it swims upward at top speed, bursts through the water, and—CHOMP!

Great White Shark

Chapter 2

A Shark's Body

Sharks have amazing bodies. Each part does a different job.

fin

eye

teeth

gills

tail

fins

Great White Shark

A shark has teeth.

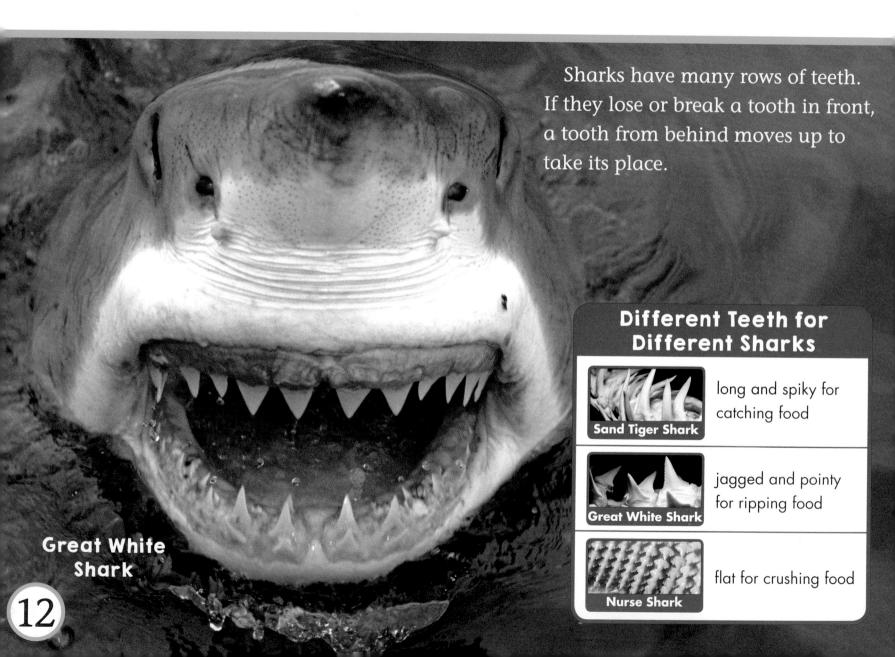

Sharks have many rows of teeth. If they lose or break a tooth in front, a tooth from behind moves up to take its place.

Great White Shark

Different Teeth for Different Sharks

Sand Tiger Shark	long and spiky for catching food
Great White Shark	jagged and pointy for ripping food
Nurse Shark	flat for crushing food

A shark has gills.

Animals need oxygen to breathe. Many get it from the air. Sharks get it from the water. The water flows over their **gills**. That's how they breathe.

gills

Whitetip Reef Shark

13

A shark has fins.

A shark's **fins** help it move, balance, and change direction. Sometimes, you can see the fin on a shark's back poking through the water!

dorsal fin

Caribbean Reef Shark

tail fins

pectoral fins

pelvic fin

Shark Alert!

A shark has skin.

ANTEATER

den

skin

the sh

rk's

Little Kids

These are denticles
up close!

Gray Nurse
Shark

A shark does not have bones!

Sharks have **cartilage** instead of bones. Cartilage bends more easily than bones do. This helps sharks twist and turn as they swim.

Your ears have cartilage. Try bending them!

This drawing of a shark shows its cartilage.

16

Chapter 3

Baby Sharks Grow Up

Baby sharks are called pups. How do they grow?

Silvertip Sharks

17

This is a shark egg.

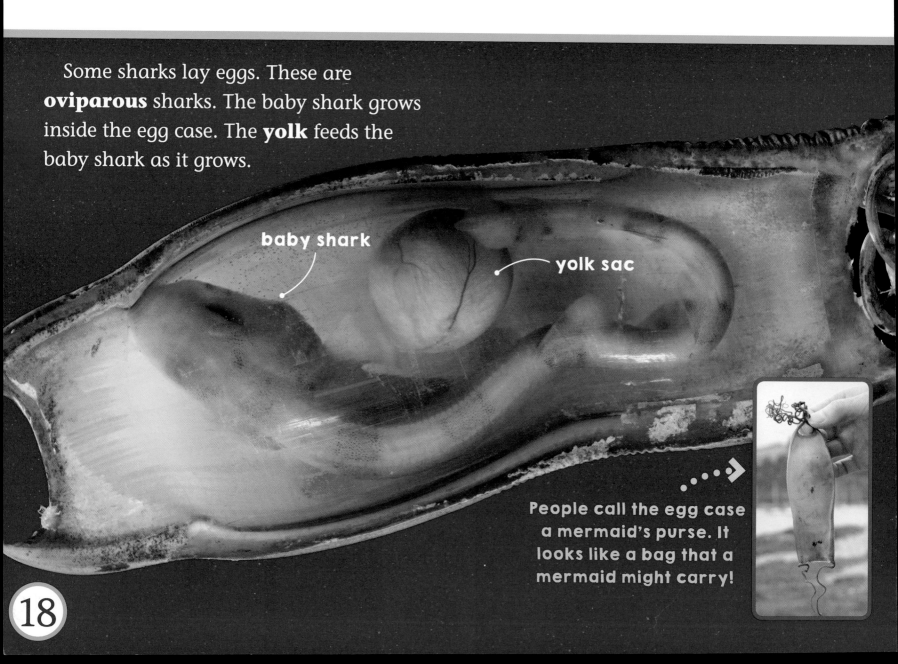

Some sharks lay eggs. These are **oviparous** sharks. The baby shark grows inside the egg case. The **yolk** feeds the baby shark as it grows.

baby shark

yolk sac

People call the egg case a mermaid's purse. It looks like a bag that a mermaid might carry!

This shark egg is hatching.

The shark pup has been inside its egg case for nine months. It breaks out by pushing against the end until it opens. Hello, world!

swell shark pup

egg case

19

This is a baby shark.

Many sharks grow inside their mothers and are born live. The pups can take care of themselves right away. They know how to swim and hunt on their own.

pup

Lemon Sharks

This shark is all grown-up!

Sharks can grow up to be different shapes, sizes, and colors. But whether they're shiny, spotted, or strange, sharks are some of the coolest fish in the sea!

Great White Shark

Cookiecutter Shark

Spotted Wobbegong

Goblin Shark

Zebra Shark

Frilled Shark

Glossary

cartilage: (kart-uh-lij)
The rubbery material that makes up a shark's skeleton

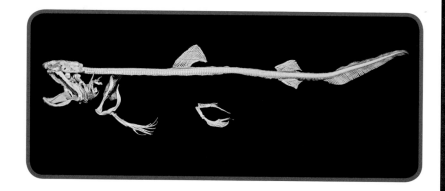

denticles:
(**dent**-ih-kuhlz)
Toothlike bumps that cover a shark's skin

fins: (finz)
The body parts that fish use to move and steer through the water

gills: (gilz) The body parts that fish use to breathe

nostril:

(**nah**-struhl) Nose holes that people and some animals use to breathe and smell

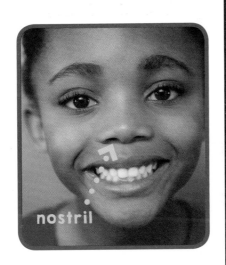

nostril

plankton: (plank-tuhn)

Tiny plants and animals that float in the ocean

oviparous: (oh-**vip**-uh-ruhss)

The name for animals that make eggs that hatch outside the mother's body

Crocodile

Swell Shark

Duck

Turtle

yolk: (yohk)

The part of an egg that feeds the baby growing inside

yolk

Index

Photos ©: cover: Image Source/Getty Images; cover background: Iness Arna/Shutterstock; back cover: Michele Westmorland/Getty Images; cover face icons and throughout: Giuseppe_R/Shutterstock; 3 reef: Irina Markova/Shutterstock; 3 shark: Krzysztof Odziomek/Shutterstock; 4 top left: wildestanimal/Shutterstock; 4 top right: Frank Greenaway/Getty Images; 4 center left: Michele Westmorland/Getty Images; 4 center right: Gino Santa Maria/Shutterstock; 4 bottom left: Kelvin Aitken/VWPics/Alamy Images; 4 bottom right: Divepic/iStockphoto; 4-5 background: Rich Carey/Shutterstock; 5 top left: IrinaK/Shutterstock; 5 center: Wayne Lynch/Getty Images; 5 bottom left: Dave Fleetham/Design Pics/Getty Images; 5 bottom right: Kelvin Aitken/SeaPics.com; 6 main: Luis Javier Sandoval/VWPICS/age fotostock; 6 inset top: Richard Koele/Dreamstime; 6 inset bottom: Rich Carey/Shutterstock; 7 main: Espen Rekdal/SeaPics.com; 7 inset: Artem Furman/Shutterstock; 8: Michael Valos/Dreamstime; 9 main: Hemis/Alamy Images; 9 inset toolbox: vtwinpixel/iStockphoto; 9 inset hammer: Floortje/iStockphoto; 9 inset saw: Sitade/iStockphoto; 10: Chris and Monique Fallows/Minden Pictures; 11: Daniela Dirscherl/WaterFrame/age fotostock; 12 main: Mike Parry/Minden Pictures; 12 inset top: Doug Perrine/SeaPics.com; 12 inset center: Doug Perrine/SeaPics.com; 12 inset bottom: Bob Cranston/SeaPics.com; 13: Konrad Wothe/Minden Pictures; 14 main: Jim Abernethy/Getty Images; 14 inset: Philip Waller/Getty Images; 15 main: Bruno Guenard/Minden Pictures; 15 inset: Alex Hyde/Minden Pictures; 16 background: Rich Carey/Shutterstock; 16 right: Arran Lewis/Dorling Kindersley/Getty Images; 16 inset: colematt/iStockphoto; 17: Mark Strickland/SeaPics.com; 18 main: Heidi and Hans-Juergen Koch/Minden Pictures; 18 inset: Kilbey/ardea.com/age fotostock; 19: Mark Conlin/VWPics/AP Images; 20: Doug Perrine/Minden Pictures; 21 main: by wildestanimal/Getty Images; 21 bottom cookiecutter: Kelvin Aitken/VWPics/Alamy Images; 21 bottom wobbegong: Fred Bavendam/Minden Pictures; 21 bottom goblin: Kelvin Aitken/VWPics/Alamy Images; 21 bottom zebra: Izanbar/Dreamstime; 21 bottom frill: Awashima Marine Park/Getty Images; 22 top left: Masa Ushioda/SeaPics.com; 22 top right: Alex Hyde/Minden Pictures; 22 bottom left: Pete Oxford/Minden Pictures; 22 bottom right: Konrad Wothe/Minden Pictures; 23 top left: Wavebreakmedia/iStockphoto; 23 top right: Napat/Shutterstock; 23 bottom left crocodile: Catchlight Lens/Shutterstock; 23 bottom left swell shark: David Kilbey/ardea.com/age fotostock; 23 bottom left duck: Jane Burton/DK Images; 23 bottom left turtle: Kerstin Hinze/Minden Pictures; 23 bottom right: Juniors Bildarchiv/age fotostock.

Library of Congress Cataloging-in-Publication Data
Names: Chanko, Pamela, 1968- author.
Title: The shark book / by Pamela Chanko.
Description: New York, NY: Children's Press®, an imprint of Scholastic Inc., 2020. | Series: Side by side | Includes index.
Identifiers: LCCN 2019004847| ISBN 9780531238417 (library binding) | ISBN 9780531246580 (paperback)
Subjects: LCSH: Sharks--Juvenile literature.
Classification: LCC QL638.9 .C43 2020 | DDC 597.3--dc23

Brought to you by the editors of *Let's Find Out*. Original Design by Marybeth Butler Rivera, Joan Michael and Judith E. Christ for Scholastic Inc.

7 8 9 10 11 12 13 14   29 28 27 26 25 24 23 22